LOVE

[AS A MANAGEMENT PRACTICE]

The Motivating Power of Love at Work

by John Earl Johnson

LOVE As A Management Practice

Published by Christian Business Men's Connection
Chattanooga, Tennessee 37414
www.cbmc.com

Printed in the United States of America
ISBN 978-1-947457-22-5
First printing
Cover design © 2019, Scott Rasmussen/Ras Graphics, Inc.

LOVE AS A MANAGEMENT PRACTICE
...never fails

By John E. Johnson

In the business and professional world, we encounter many "secrets" for effective management. Rarely, however, do we find one that is guaranteed to work.

"Love" is not a word we often use in board and conference rooms, offices, cafeterias or watercoolers. But there is no justification for that if it's properly understood and utilized.

The world commonly portrays love as a feeling or sensation: emotional, fleeting, fluctuating, unpredictable and self-centered. In contrast, God commands His believers to love as a deliberate decision for the benefit of others, caringly introducing them to His Son, the author of love...Jesus Christ. As the Scriptures tell us, God is love – and where love is, God is there, changing hearts.

A lawyer and member of the Pharisees, seeking to test Jesus, asked, "Teacher, which is the greatest commandment in the Law?" (Of the more than 900 laws the religious leaders had compiled.) Jesus answered, "You shall love the Lord your God with all your heart, and with all your soul, and with all your mind. This is the greatest and foremost commandment. The second is like it, 'You shall love your neighbor as yourself.' On these two commandments depend the whole Law and the Prophets" (Matthew 22:36-40).

The question arises: What is this love? We find the answer in 1 Corinthians 13:4-7. It says:

> *"Love is patient, love is kind, love does not envy, love is not proud, love is not rude, love is not self-seeking, love keeps no record of wrongs, love does not delight in evil but love rejoices in the truth, love always protects, love always hopes, love always perseveres and **love never fails**."*

Why does this matter? Because Jesus often spoke about love, and His followers are exhorted to love in many other New Testament passages. Here are some of them:

"LOVE ONE ANOTHER" (John 13:34a)

"LOVE ONE ANOTHER" (John 13:35)

"LOVE ONE ANOTHER " (John 15:12)

"LOVE ONE ANOTHER" (John 15:17)

"LOVE ONE ANOTHER" (Romans 13:8)

"MAKE YOUR LOVE INCREASE" (1 Thessalonians 3:12)

"LOVE EACH OTHER" (1 Thessalonians 4:9)

"LOVE ONE ANOTHER DEEPLY" (1 Peter 3:8)

"LOVE EACH OTHER DEEPLY" (1 Peter 4:8)

"LOVE ONE ANOTHER" (1 John 3:11)

"LOVE ONE ANOTHER" (1 John 3:23)

"LOVE ONE ANOTHER" (1 John 4:7)

"LOVE ONE ANOTHER" (1 John 4:11)

"LOVE ONE ANOTHER" (1 John 4:12)

"LOVE ONE ANOTHER" (2 John 5)

Clearly, God considers our love – for Himself and for one another – of great importance. Not one of these passages suggests, "except in the marketplace," so we have every reason to believe that love – in the biblical understanding of the word – is just as important where we work as anywhere else.

In the following sections, we will see *Love As a Management Practice*, how it works and why it works.

LOVE AS A MANAGEMENT PRACTICE

INTRODUCTION: LOVE NEVER FAILS

SUPPORT:

When we read in 1 Corinthians 13:8 that "love never fails," a reasonable question is, what does that mean? It could also be translated, "love is unfailing." For help, we find Webster's Dictionary provides this partial definition for **Love**: "unselfish loyal and benevolent concern for the good of another, the fatherly concern of God for man."

As for **Unfailing**, the same dictionary says this: "constant, unflagging, everlasting, sure, inexhaustible." Putting the definitions for love and unfailing together, we get a very different picture of what love truly is, compared to what popular culture tells us.

Later in the 13th chapter of 1 Corinthians, it makes the intriguing statement, "And now these three remain: faith, hope and love. But the greatest of these is love." Why is love called "the greatest"? Our goal in this study is to find the answer to this, as well as why we're told, "love never fails." Leading up to this, consider what 1 Corinthians 13:1-3 has to say:

> *"If I speak in the tongues of men or of angels, but do not have love, I am only a resounding gong or a clanging cymbal. If I have the gift of prophecy and can fathom all mysteries and all knowledge, and if I have a faith that can move mountains, but do not have love, I am nothing. If I give all I possess to the poor and give over my body to hardship that I may boast, but do not have love, I gain nothing."*

Before proceeding, consider what a couple more verses have to say about love, as well as two useful quotations. Galatians 5:13 says we are to "serve one another in love." After listing a number of admirable qualities like compassion, kindness, humility, gentleness and patience, Colossians admonishes, "over all these virtues put on love, which binds them all together in perfect unity."

"Service is love made visible," according to an anonymous source, and author Hank Hanegraaff says, "without choice, love is meaningless."

APPLICATION:

Love: Actions Speak Louder Than Words

Noted British author and Christian apologist C.S. Lewis was addressing the importance of love in action when he wrote, "Next to the Blessed Sacrament itself, your neighbor is the holiest object presented to your senses."

As Christians we are urged to share our hope in Jesus Christ, but in many instances the people we encounter are more influenced by the way we treat them (love them) than by our eloquence (words). Only a small percentage of us are word-gifted as persuasive evangelists, but we are all capable of showing the love of Christ through our actions.

In the work world, discussions about faith are typically limited to outside the parameters of the job. They are regarded as highly personal, easily trespassed upon, and in some places, illegal. However, there are no barriers to loving those with whom we work. When love is incorporated into management practices, then God is on the job changing hearts. Because where love is, God is. Genuine love is practiced in many ways but always intended to benefit those receiving it.

All organizations are human and therefore, relational

On this earthbound journey of unpredictable success and failure, it is a supernatural act to access heavenly advice about a human practice that cannot fail. Other than the Bible's claim about salvation, I know of no other strategy or tactic making the "cannot fail" promise. We can acquire this Godly attribute through ceaseless prayer and practice, so we can demonstrate it without discrimination to those around us.

CONCLUSION:

Win/Win

God prescribes love in terms of the specific actions and attitudes described in 1 Corinthians 13, so we can practice it with our fellow humans, blessing both those upon whom it is practiced and those who practice it. In this life we will practice it imperfectly, but in heaven, the believer will receive perfect love.

QUESTIONS:

1. We cited the phrase, "love never fails," from 1 Corinthians 13. In your opinion, what does this mean? Does it ring true for you?

2. In reality, we all have failed people that we loved – and people we love have failed us. So how can we apply the "love never fails" principle in the workplace and in our everyday interactions with colleagues and customers, as well as with friends and family?

3. Describe an incident when demonstrating love worked for you, or when being the recipient of love had a positive effect on you. Have you ever experienced "love at work" in a working environment? If so, what did that look like?

1

MANAGEMENT PRACTICE:
LOVE IS PATIENT

SUPPORT:

Webster's on **Patience**: "not hasty or impetuous, bearing pain or trials calmly, without complaint." **Impatience**: "irritated by delay or opposition."

Scriptures: "A person's wisdom yields patience; it is one's glory to overlook an offense" (Proverbs 19:11). "Through patience a ruler can be persuaded" (Proverbs 25:15).

Expressed in straight-forward terms, Patience is listening for understanding.

APPLICATION:

A good place to start Note that "Patience" heads the list of behaviors for demonstrating God's love to others. Who does not endlessly benefit from God's patience with our foolishness?

Patience and its antithesis, Impatience, permeate manager/employee relations, particularly when expectations become frustrated. Such as when timelines are missed, mistakes are made, unforeseen obstacles arise, cost overruns occur, etc. In situations like these, for a manager to react with impatience is considered normal and expected; to react with patience is abnormal and unexpected.

Impatience is thinly disguised anger. Being impatient instantly communicates disappointment and dissatisfaction with the "guilty" party. Does it work? Yes, creating fear and intimidation works – short term. Long term it develops anxiety and discourages undertaking any independent initiatives with any potential for failure.

Management's role is to solve problems Anything worth attaining is _always_ difficult to obtain. Every worthwhile attainment, like gold, is well-fortified, stubbornly resisting the efforts of its seekers. Success favors patient persistence.

That is to say, managers are paid to overcome, at the hands of those they supervise, the inevitable obstacles to achieving worthwhile goals. To become impatient when things go wrong by directly or indirectly laying blame on subordinates wastes valuable time, forcing employees to become defensive and argumentative. What is needed instead is an open and honest description of the problem by the person or persons closest to the situation. It has been said that Bill Gates wanted bad news first and fastest. This means he wanted his people to courageously present, as soon as possible, problems better solved with his participation. It also implies that he will be available as needed – but it better be worth his time.

Patience introduces Rx to a situation Patience provides the margin that recognizes mistakes will be made and encourages initiative, openness, honesty and clarity about situations. It's a prescription that avoids wasting time on excuses. Patience welcomes hesitant or indecisive parties to fearlessly participate with others as they anticipate the unlocking of new solutions to the situation.

Patience contributes to the 'Genius of Objectivity' As a management consultant, I concluded that I couldn't possibly know as much about the details of a situation as the client immersed in it. However, since they were so closely involved in the process, often they had lost all patience and objectivity. To quote the clichés, they became "buried in the trees having lost sight of the forest," or were "up to one's hips in alligators having lost sight of the objective to drain the swamp."

My approach dealt with positive, purpose-driven questions relating to the original objectives, which had been confirmed by the answer to: "Why is that important and how is that measured?"

Here are some suggested questions you could ask that apply patience to problems presented by stumped employees. Note: These questions should _always_ be preceded by a silent prayer for wisdom:

- What are you attempting to accomplish? Why is that important/how is it measured?

- What still needs to be done? Why is that important/how is it measured?

- What would you like from me? Why is that important for you?

- What will you do, now we have talked? Why is that important?

Drill down by repeatedly asking, "why is that important/how can it be measured?" to eliminate symptoms and come to the truth of the matter. Make the above line of inquiry clear to your employees, so they can be better prepared before approaching you for advice.

CONCLUSION:

Patience produces better solutions faster

As a believer, the Christian manager is God's representative on the job. Applying patience to situations is not only God's imperative but also brings God's wisdom to bear on the solution. If you attempt to prayerfully apply patience to situations, you will come up with better solutions faster, while at the same time making a goodwill investment in the people you manage.

QUESTIONS:

1. What are some kinds of situations that make you feel impatient?

2. Who or what kinds of people make you impatient?

3. In both cases, what is your plan for overcoming impatience and to intentionally strive to implement and practice patience?

MANAGEMENT PRACTICE:
LOVE IS KIND

SUPPORT:

Webster's on **Kindness**: "disposed to be helpful and solicitous, a self-restraining nature, to give pleasure or relief, agreeable." **Unkindness**: "harsh, cruel, unsympathetic, and unhelpful."

Scriptures: "Thus He shows for all time the tremendous generosity of the grace and kindness He has expressed towards us in Christ Jesus" (Ephesians 2:7, Phillips translation).

"Be merciful in action, kindly in heart, humble in mind. *Accept life*, be most patient and tolerant with one another " (Colossians 3:12-13, Phillips).

APPLICATION:

'Patience' and 'Kindness' call for different behaviors Patience is situational, inspiring calming behavior when things go awry. Kindness is general, behaving with a constant, caring, constructive attitude to those around you.

God made employees, and men made enterprises; serving the former serves the latter God is not likely to judge our earthly contributions to balance sheets and profit & loss statements, but rather how we cared for the people He brought to us. Nevertheless, as institutional caretakers, we are ordered to submit to human authority: "be subject for the Lord's sake to every human institution" (1 Peter 2:13). Institutions of every sort are relational collectives offering opportunities to serve those whom we would otherwise never meet. People treated kindly do a better job.

To your people, it's all personal Employees arrive at work with a full agenda of relationally meaningful lives, their jobs being just one of their priorities. In the reality TV program, "Undercover Boss," the CEO disguised as a trainee would uncover significant personal needs, for which the company can provide real help. As the episodes showed, this resulted in grateful, more loyal, and likely, more productive employees.

'The score takes care of itself' Bill Walsh, late Hall of Fame head coach for the San Francisco 49ers and Stanford lecturer, wrote a book entitled, *The Score Takes Care of Itself*. Its main premise was that when you concentrate on servicing your people by instructing and encouraging their individual best performances as contributing team members, they will naturally produce the best overall outcome for the enterprise they represent.

KINDNESS ISN'T JUST A NICE NOTION – IT'S SOUND SCIENCE

The Healing Power of Kindness by Lloyd Dean & James Doty, M.D.

This extensive scientific literature review, sponsored by *Dignity Health* and conducted by the Center for Compassion and Altruism Research and Education (CCARE) at Stanford University, revealed a growing body of scientific evidence that indicates kindness holds the power to heal. We now know this often overlooked, virtually cost-free remedy has a significant, measurable impact on our physical health.

For example, the positive effect of kindness is even greater than that of taking aspirin to reduce the risk of a heart attack. And it doesn't even require a trip to the pharmacy. The review also found that patients aren't the only ones who see better results from kind treatment -- the doctors, nurses, and caregivers who provide the kind treatment are beneficiaries as well.

CONCLUSION:

Kindness 'Kustomized' To be appropriately kind to your coworkers, you need to get to know them as workplace family. Getting to know them entails personality assessment tools as well as face-to-face dialogue about their passions, ambitions, strengths and weaknesses. In the "Undercover Boss," this is shown through the sharing of life stories. In one situation, a part-time student employee amazingly revealed that he and about 20% of his 1,000-person minority high school were homeless, sleeping in cars and under culverts. This interaction led to substantial help being given to many of the students.

QUESTIONS:

1. Do you feel that you have an in-depth understanding of those closest to you (including family)? Do you know what motivates – and demotivates - them?

2. Which of these people do you think need better understanding?

3. What steps can you take for understanding them better? (There is a free online version of the Meyers-Briggs personal assessment test. Do you think that would be helpful?)

3

MANAGEMENT PRACTICE:
LOVE DOES NOT ENVY

SUPPORT:

Webster's on **Envy**: "Painful or resentful awareness of an advantage enjoyed by another, joined with a desire to possess the same advantage." Here are some things the Scriptures have to say about Envy:

Scriptures: "And I saw that all toil and all achievement spring from one person's envy of another. This too is meaningless, a chasing after the wind" (Ecclesiastes 4:4). "A heart at peace gives life to the body, but envy rots the bones" (Proverbs 14:30). "For where you have envy and selfish ambition, there you find disorder and every evil practice" (James 3:16).

Writing on this topic, author and pastor Charles Swindoll observed, "When you compare beyond your God-given capabilities, then you can expect frustration, discouragement, mediocrity, and, in the long run, defeat. Cultivate your capabilities. Stop comparing. ***Enjoy being you!***"

APPLICATION:

Envy is rooted in unrewarded, counterfeit love In other words, this is love of another's possessions or love of another's status. Very few people have everything they want, and the organizations they work for offer plenty to envy: titles, parking spots, workspaces, expense accounts, wages, etc.

Apple founder Steve Jobs stated, "Your time is limited, so don't waste it living someone else's life." To counter the tendency for envy, including distracted, unrealistic, wishful thinking, the manager would be wise to install a personalized productivity system, with the focus on increasing individual contributions. This would leave everyone focused on improving their output rather than looking "over the fence" and viewing themselves in comparison to others.

Personal/Team Productivity According to the authors of *First, Break All The Rules,* knowing what's expected of an employee is more than a job description. It's a detailed understanding of how what one person produces helps to increase team productivity. Which fits with the company's reasons-for-being, in terms of customer deliverables and profitability, and helps employees to recognize their valued contributions.

CONCLUSION

The Antidote to Envy – Focus on Contribution Maximizing productivity involves putting the right people in the right places, doing the right things. The following helps in establishing a needed focus on contribution. "How measured?" clarifies intention, provides actionable feedback and determines achievement.

QUESTIONS:
Please answer the following for the organization you represent:

ENTERPRISE PURPOSE:
Why does my organization benefit its customers?
How is this measured?

WORK GROUP CONTRIBUTION:
Why does my work group contribute to enterprise purpose?
How is this measured?

PERSONAL CONTRIBUTION
Why do I contribute to my work group's purpose?
How is this measured?

Enterprise structure can be a major impediment to change W. Edwards Deming, an esteemed engineer and management consultant, observed that more than 90% of the barriers to change in an organization are the systems of that organization, not the people in it, who feel powerless to deal with the systems.

Stephen Covey, author of *The 7 Habits of Highly Effective People*, wrote, "you are perfectly aligned for the results you get." That is to say, whatever happens, good or bad, could be predicted if you understood the structure and culture of the company.

4

MANAGEMENT PRACTICE:
LOVE IS NOT PROUD

SUPPORT:

Webster's on **Pride**: "inordinate self-esteem, conceit, congratulating oneself." It defines Humility as "a spirit of deference or submission." The Bible has much to say about humility and the humble. Here are just a few examples:

Scriptures: "God opposes the proud, but shows favor to the humble" (James 4:6). "The Lord detests the proud of heart...they will not go unpunished" (Proverbs 16:5) Even Jesus said, "If I testify about myself, my testimony is not true" (John 5:31).

APPLICATION:

Pride Separates, Contribution Unites The Bible has nothing good to say about human pride. In fact, it reveals how it can lead to a confrontation with God about who's in charge – and we all know how that turns out. Pride substitutes self-acclaim for God's acclaim. Pride is love turned inward, whereas God commands us to turn love outward. Alcoholics Anonymous, claims one step to recovery lies in "service." In other words, directing one's attention outward by serving others in practical ways.

Pride is satisfaction in being 'useful' to others Being useful in a work setting starts with a detailed understanding of what a worker is expected to contribute, along with constant feedback about measured progress to that end. In any organization, the employee's ultimate "usefulness" lies in helping to fulfill the organization's mission. This happens by delivering measurable customer benefits in a cost-effective manner.

CONCLUSION:

Pride in the outcome contributes to the enterprise's mission An old story illustrates contribution as it relates to mission: Three stonecutters working in a quarry were asked to describe their job. The first replied, "I am cutting stone." The second answered, "I am cutting stone to make its dimensions uniform to fit exactly in a wall." The third answered, "I am building a cathedral." What a difference perspective can make!

Each employee should be able to identify and connect his/her contributions to the organization's ultimate reasons-for-being.

QUESTIONS:

1. Can you think of a time – or times – when you saw that pride could be a destructive, disunifying force? What were the effects that you observed?

2. Are there ways, in your opinion, that pride can be a positive, motivating influence? Explain your answer.

3. Why do we typically find humility to be such an admirable trait? Who can you think of that is a truly humble individual – how is their humility manifested?

Do this daily Admiring others is practicing humility by focusing one's attention outward rather than inward. Make a practice of encouraging fellow employees each day as follows:

1. Compliment for Action, by name and specific action taken: "Mary, I noticed you worked late to get that order out. Thank you. You perfectly reflect our commitment to customer service."

2. Compliment for Attitude, which is even more important than an action: "Bill, we didn't win that one, but your effort was a great example for the team to go forward."

3. Compliment at home: "Jane, your volunteer efforts show your heart for others."

4. Other examples of how to encourage and uplift others could include:

    • *"Thank you for...."*

    • *"I couldn't have gotten this done without you."*

    • *"Your generosity is an example for me."*

    • *"You bring a unique contribution to our team by...."*

    • *"I would like to brainstorm some ideas with you."*

A WORD OF CAUTION: "Flattery" is quickly detected as false and manipulative, having the opposite effect of genuine commendation.

5

MANAGEMENT PRACTICE:
LOVE IS NOT RUDE (IGNORANT)

SUPPORT:

Webster's on **Rudeness**: "offensive in manner or action, discourteous, vulgar, forceful, abrupt, ignorance." **Respect**: "considerate of other people."

Scriptures: "He is able to deal gently with those who are ignorant and are going astray, since he himself is subject to weakness" (Hebrews 5:2). "For it is God's will that by doing good you should silence the ignorant talk of foolish people" (1 Peter 2:15).

APPLICATION:

Raising Relational IQ Every organization functions relationally, relying on cooperation among its employees. Cooperation means many things, one of which is demonstrating mutual respect. Rude behavior is disrespectful, igniting justifiable anger and possible retribution. Obviously, that does not enhance relationships.

Codes of Conduct: *"I did what?!"* One excuse for rudeness can be ignorance of relational codes of conduct. The remedy for this is a clear understanding of how we, the people of this enterprise, are to behave toward one another, as we work together to get things done. Where there are no common codes of conduct, interpersonal conflicts tend to come down to, "He said, she said." And the outcome most often favors the more powerful party.

Netflix, in a comprehensive culture statement, recommends as one behavior, "You say what you think, even if it is controversial." This could be considered rude behavior, but it comes with a caveat: Offering alternative suggestions should never be personal. Rather, they should always be presented in search of a better solution.

Organizational Cultures of Respect Are Not Natural
People arrive at work with a variety of attitudes and sensitivities, many of which carry the potential to offend or be offended. Sustainably positive work environments are not natural, but always the result of a managed culture.

Do you think that the consistently good service you get in a restaurant, supermarket or bank is due to the spontaneous goodwill of its servers? No way. Behind consistently great service you will always find culturally dedicated management and a continuously well-trained staff.

CONCLUSION:

Rudeness must be addressed because:

- *Rudeness is bad behavior*

- *Bad behavior undermines relationships*

- *Relationships are vital to effective teamwork*

- *Effective teamwork maximizes productivity*

Most rude behavior is spur-of-the-moment and unconscious;

often the offense occurs in the eye of the beholder. Because of this, the manager needs to regularly and publicly deputize everyone to call out negative behavior to the offender, as specifically and non-confrontationally as possible. Here are some suggested steps:

- **Request a private dialogue**
  "I need your advice on something important."

- **Describe, without judgment, the behavior occurring**
  "In meeting 'X,' you talked over me while I was saying...."

- **Describe your assumptions based on that behavior**
  "I took that to mean...what I had to say was not important."

- **Describe how that behavior affects you emotionally**
  "I felt minimized, embarrassed and I shut down."

- **Describe your needs, and how they differed from what occurred**
  "When invited to a meeting and having an opinion, I need to be heard."

- **Describe a plan of action – what are we going to do?**
  "When I give input in a meeting, *before you respond*, could you repeat whatever it is you heard me say?"

QUESTIONS:

1. How is your organization's code of conduct enforced and reinforced?

2. If no corporate code currently exists, does your work group have one? If so, is it used – and how?

3. How do you manage appropriate and inappropriate conduct? How does everyone gain a common understanding of expected behaviors and responses?

6

MANAGEMENT PRACTICE:
LOVE IS NOT SELF-SEEKING (SELFISH)

SUPPORT:

Webster's on **Self-Seeking**: "the act or practice of selfishly advancing one's ends." **Teamwork**: "subordinating personal prominence to the efficiency of the whole." **Cooperation**: "mutual benefits outweigh those gained by personal competition."

Scriptures: "Do nothing from selfishness or empty conceit, but with humility of mind regard one another as more important than yourselves; do not merely look out for your own personal interests, but also for the interests of others" (Philippians 2:3,4).

APPLICATION:

Self-Seeking Is Contagious Self-seeking attitudes result in influencing others to respond in kind by reinforcing their own self-interests, thereby inflicting cross-purposes within the team. To offset the tendency for selfishness, the manager needs to instill a contribution-centered set of needs greater than self.

The U.S. Marine Corps magnificently displays this in their corporate commitment: "Find the willpower you never knew you had, the strength you never knew you needed, bonds that will never break, and a lifelong desire to serve a purpose far greater than self." This is promised to create mental, physical, relational and purpose-driven superiority in those willing to yield their self-centered authority to the higher authority of the USMC.

Ask Not What Your Company Can Do For You, Ask ... An historic example of supplanting self-centered love with service-centered love occurred when President John F. Kennedy, in his inaugural address, challenged fellow citizens to, "Ask not what your country can do for you; ask what you can do for your country." More than 50 years later, this powerful challenge to contribute still motivates Americans to sacrificially serve the needs of others through the benevolent leadership of the Peace Corps.

CONCLUSION:

Self-seeking is natural; serving (loving) others is learned Creating mutually beneficial servant relationships in an organization is more than a job description. It's a detailed understanding of how one person's output serves and supports coworker's efforts in fulfilling the organization's mission. This relationship is determined by asking fellow workers: "What do you need from me to do your job with excellence? When do you need it? And in what form?" This should be followed up by regularly asking, "How am I doing?" (Peter Drucker, *The Effective Executive*).

This process identifies interdependent teammate relationships throughout the organization. Perhaps equally important, it also identifies where no demand exists for an interactive teamwork relationship.

Teamwork Evaluation

Have coworkers rate themselves then others on the following "teamwork" criteria:

Employee ...Self (or Teammate)   *Rate*
10 (BEST) - 1(NONE)

- Straight forward and above board, no hidden agenda   _____

- Risks by exposing ideas, reactions and feelings to the team   _____

- Respects and accepts feedback from team members   _____

- Presses for information when others appear to withhold   _____

- Prepares beforehand, follows up afterward   _____

- Provides direct input to help me do my job better   _____

- Challenges self and team to get better   _____

- Works hard to understand the thoughts and feelings of others _____

QUESTIONS:

1. Where and why do your self-scores differ from how teammates score you?

2. What can you do – or what will you do – to address those differences?

MANAGEMENT PRACTICE:
LOVE KEEPS NO RECORD OF WRONGS

(in other words, FORGIVENESS)

SUPPORT:

Webster's on **Forgiveness**: "cease to feel resentments against an offender, give up claim or retaliation."

Scriptures: "'Lord, how often will my brother sin against me, and I forgive him? As many as seven times?' Jesus said to him, 'I do not say to you seven times, but seventy-seven times'" (Matthew 18:21-22). "Blessed is the one whose sin the Lord will never count against them" (Romans 4:8).

The esteemed publication *Psychology Today* had this to say in an article entitled, "The Nature of Forgiveness": "Mustering up genuine compassion for those who have wronged us, instead of allowing anger toward them to eat away at us, is the course of action recommended by most psychologists. When you forgive someone, you make the choice to give up your desire for revenge and feelings of resentment. You also stop judging the person who caused you the hurt. Instead of revenge, resentment, and judgment, you show generosity, compassion, and kindness. In forgiveness, you don't forget that the offense occurred, nor do you excuse it. You substitute your negative with positive feelings, thoughts, and behavior."

APPLICATION:

Sinning injures, forgiveness heals We all sin by omission (should do) or commission (should not do), and all have the potential to offend or be offended. When sinned against, as an alternative to becoming helpless victims, we can proactively decide to forgive rather than wallow in the collateral damage caused by another's bad behavior. Romans 12:19 commands, "leave revenge to the Lord."

Forgiveness is self-initiated, coming before confrontation. It allows us time to reflect on our injury, along with the part we may have played (rarely are we 100% innocent). So having already forgiven, the act of confrontation is for the benefit of the perpetrator, who may not realize the injurious impact of his or her behavior. Importantly, this primary healing act of forgiveness is self-initiated, and not tied to acceptance by the perpetrator, who may be in full denial – or may refuse to ask for forgiveness.

For a model for how to approach confrontation in a positive, constructive manner, see the example included earlier in #5 MANAGEMENT PRACTICE: LOVE IS NOT RUDE (IGNORANT).

Confronting Yourself It is widely believed that "hurt people hurt people." So when the Holy Spirit convicts us of sin, we immediately seek forgiveness. The very act of requesting forgiveness, first from God and then from another, clears our conscience. As Psalm 32:5 declares, "I will confess my transgressions to the Lord,' and You forgave the iniquity of my sin."

Institute in Basic Life Principles on "How to ask for forgiveness":

- It takes a lot of courage to make yourself vulnerable, but it is worth it

- Involve no others, confess in private to the person you offended

- Avoid details, briefly identify your offense. For instance, disloyalty, dishonesty, etc.

- Do not rationalize: "I did this because...."

- Do not mention other people's involvement

- This is not the time to share your faith

- Consider rejection, nevertheless proceed. It's the right thing to do

- Clear your conscience as soon as possible

- Face to face is good, but a telephone call keeps it briefer

QUESTIONS:

1. Are there unresolved offenses that someone has against you?

2. Do you have unresolved offenses that you have against others?

3. What is your plan for addressing (and resolving) those records of wrongs that could be having a negative impact on your relationships?

MANAGEMENT PRACTICE: LOVE DOES NOT DELIGHT IN EVIL, BUT REJOICES IN THE TRUTH

SUPPORT:

Webster's on **Truth**: "a body of true statements and propositions supported by facts." **Evil**: "perverts/falsifies the truth."

Scriptures: "The one whose walk is blameless, who does what is righteous, speaks the truth from their heart" (Psalm 15:2). "An honest witness tells the truth, but a false witness tells lies" (Proverbs 12:17). "Buy the truth and do not sell it – wisdom, instruction and insight as well" (Proverbs 23:23). In His prayer to God the Father, Jesus asked, "sanctify them by the truth; your word is truth" (John 17:17).

APPLICATION:

Truth & Evil in Organizational Life: building a culture of truth It is not possible to remove all temptations for evil from among the people of an organization. What may be possible is to build a culture built on truth, so that when employee judgment, or behavior, runs contrary to the truth, the truth backed by facts can be presented in a self-correcting way. Employees in such an environment will come to accept, trust and deal in the truth. If they can't operate in an environment of truth, honesty and integrity, they will depart.

Truth is a Matter of Facts

- Truth consists of facts. Facts are measurable, so truth is measurable

- Truth is revealed to anyone willing to search for it, and it can set you free

- Truth can be built on; the truth is reliable and works every time

- The higher up the organization, the greater the consequences of truth and evil, which includes ignorance of truth

Truth may be discovered by asking: "Why is that important?" followed by, "And how is that measured?" Consultant Gerry Faust said, "If you want things to change, measure them."

TRUTH & EVIL IN ORGANIZATIONAL LIFE

Four categories generally represent an organization's reason for being, and each can be supported by the truth, as revealed by facts. Evil falsifies or ignores the truth.

- **Customers**

   Truth: No organization survives without satisfied customers

   Facts: Satisfied customers are repeat users. Satisfied customers recommend your products/services. Satisfied customers are loyal; when dissatisfied, they complain to get it right rather than depart. Customers are satisfied if your product or service adds perceived value to their reason for being. (See customer satisfaction criteria at the end of this segment.)

Evil/Ignorance of the Truth: This is to assume your customers are satisfied without consciously striving to verify it.

- **Profitability**

Truth: No organization can survive unless financially sound.

Facts: Financial health is determined by an array of measurable facts. Some more significant than others: Cash flow/AR/AP. Every employee needs to know how their organization makes and loses money, then how their job and how they perform it makes and loses money. Armed with the truth, employees can self-adjust to make more and lose less for the organization they serve.

Evil/Ignorance of the Truth: This is to assume that others are solely responsible for the financial health of the organization.

- **Productivity**

Truth: Productivity is the return on invested resources. Equipment and systems have limited range of returns, whereas human capital and potential is unlimited.

Facts: Overall productivity is calculable: sales per employee, the gross/net profit per employee, and the return on assets/equity/earnings compared to industry averages.

Productivity challenges apply to what management expert Peter Drucker called "Knowledge Workers": employees largely self-managed, determining their priorities and tasks. They are valuable because their contribution, unconstrained by tactical systems, can potentially expand the organization's mission by thinking and acting strategically. And that is how the truth of their productivity is judged – by original and measurable contributions to the enterprise's Mission.

Evil/Ignorance of the Truth: This pertains to management's failure to follow up and measurably verify expectations in a timely manner.

- **Employee Attraction/Retention:**

Truth: Successful organizations keep and attract the best people.

Facts: No organization survives without the talent, motivation and cooperation of its employees. Proper care of employees results in satisfied customers and successful companies. Facts identifying employee welfare include low turnover, contributions to suggestion plans, morale surveys, voluntary worker feedback, customer feedback, new employment applications, and harmony in the workforce as perceived internally and externally. Employees are generally satisfied when they and the organizations they serve are growing.

Evil/Ignorance of the Truth: This involves management's failure to personally engage and track employee satisfaction and personal progress.

CONCLUSION:

The search for truth never ends Starting at the top, everyone is accountable for the advancement of truth in the enterprise they serve. This should include verifiable improvement in employee relations, customer satisfaction, productivity and profitability.

THE most powerful marketing force: CUSTOMER ENDORSEMENT Customers voluntarily promote, with increasing (+) levels of conviction, your products/services IF they benefit from four cumulative service deliverables:

+   **ACCURACY**: delivered as promised (on time, as ordered)

++   **AVAILABILITY**: at my convenience (think ATM)

+++   **ADVOCACY**: assists my personal interests (furthers me)

++++   **EDUCATION**: teaches me self-reliance (do-it-yourself)
(reference, *First Break All the Rules*)

To Survey/Assess Customer Relationships, Ask:

1.   Why did you start doing business with us?

2.   What do you like most about our relationship?

3.   What do you dislike most in our relationship?

4.   What changes would you like to see in our relationship?

5.   If you left for a competitor, what would the reason be?

QUESTIONS:

1.   Why are your customers satisfied? Are they satisfied – how do you know?

2.   Why are your employees satisfied? Are they satisfied – how do you know?

3,   Why are you financially stable? Are you financially stable?

4.   Why are you more productive than competitors? Are you more productive – how do you know?

9

MANAGEMENT PRACTICE: LOVE ALWAYS PROTECTS

SUPPORT:

Webster's on **Protects**: "to shield from injury, support one that is smaller/weaker." **Prepares**: "to make ready for some purpose."

C.S. Lewis, in *The Problem of Pain*, writes, "Try to exclude the possibility of suffering which the order of nature and the existence of free-wills involve, and you find that you have excluded life itself...pain insists on being attended to. God whispers to us in our pleasures, but shouts in our pain; it is his megaphone to rouse a deaf world."

Scriptures: "'For I know the plans I have for you,' declares the Lord, 'plans to prosper you and not to harm you, plans to give you hope and a future'" (Jeremiah 29:11). "For to you it has been granted for Christ's sake, not only to believe in Him, but also to suffer for His sake" (Philippians 1:29). "Jesus knew that the Father had put all things under His power" (John 13:3).

APPLICATION:

Mission Accomplished, Sacrifices Included Our greatest example of love is God the Father's love for his Son, Jesus Christ.

But when God commissioned His Son to save mankind, He did not "protect" Him from personal tests of deprivation, temptation, torment, betrayal, and ultimately, merciless execution. These trials He endured for the greater purpose of the mission: to pay the price for past, present and future sins of mankind, offering the solution and salvation to those who accept Christ's sacrifice for our sins.

The Father entrusted His Son to do the job, sacrifices included. The "protection" Jesus could count on was that God the Father could always be relied on: "I am not alone, for My Father is with Me...." "Do you think I cannot call on my Father, and He will put at my disposal more than 12 legions of angels?" (John 16:32; Matthew 26:53).

Jesus "protects" His followers by bestowing on them the eternal gift of salvation and the permanent installation of the Holy Spirit, directly linking each of us to the triune God and heaven hereafter.

Best Protected Is Best Prepared To protect people under your authority, one of the most loving things you can do is to prepare them for the challenges that lie ahead. Challenges that are inevitable, but not yet obvious to one less experienced. The best-prepared employees will embrace and overcome obstacles on the path to success, thanks to their obedience and the self-confidence you instilled in them by training. Hebrews 5:8 speaks of Jesus in this way: "Son though he was, he learned obedience from what he suffered."

Trouble Tests Commitment, Character and Courage The Bible says in this life we will always have trouble, much of it self-inflicted. "For all have sinned and fall short of the glory of God" (Romans 3:23). Troubles represent challenges to overcome on the path to accomplishment; troubles test commitment, character and courage. Some troubles have an eternal purpose by driving us to our knees. It is said the majority of people come to faith early in their life; later they likely come under duress, motivated by the troubles they cannot control.

Managers best "protect" their employees by instilling in them attitudes of service and contribution. Both of these serve them well in every aspect of life, including how they perceive their work and carry out their responsibilities.

HOW TO 'PROTECT' YOUR PEOPLE

The best "Protected" employees understand where and how they fit in as contributors to the organization. As in Management Practice #6: Love is not self-seeking, here is a formula that helps put in perspective how to prepare and thus Protect your people as valuable employees:

1. Organizations are designed to serve their customers:

   - *What does my organization achieve with excellence? How is it measured?*
   - *Why do customers benefit from this achievement? How is it measured?*

2. Operational functions serve their organization as follows:

   - *What does my operational group achieve with excellence? How is it measured?*
   - *Why does my organization benefit from this achievement? How is it measured?*

3. Employees serve their coworkers as follows:

   - *What in my job do I achieve with excellence? How is it measured?*
   - *Why do my coworkers benefit from this achievement? How is it measured?*

4. Personally how can I improve my contribution to coworkers:

   - *In what ways can my personal job performance improve? How is it measured?*

- *How will my coworkers rate the effect on them? How is this measured?*

QUESTIONS:

1. Are the people you manage aware of the considerations above?

2. If not, how will you go about correcting the situation so these questions can be used for both personal and organizational evaluation?

3. How will you measure progress as you move forward?

10

MANAGEMENT PRACTICE: LOVE ALWAYS HOPES

SUPPORT:

Webster's on **Hope**: "to cherish a desire with expectations of fulfillment, someone upon whom hopes are centered."

Scriptures: "The eyes of the Lord are on those who fear him, on those whose hope is in his unfailing love" (Psalm 33:18). "Yes, my soul, find rest in God; my hope comes from him" (Psalm 62:5). "Christ in you the hope of glory" (Colossians 1:27). "May the God of hope fill you with all joy and peace as you trust in him, so that you may overflow with hope by the power of the Holy Spirit" (Romans 15:13).

APPLICATION:

To the world, 'hope' is not a strategy – but for us it is
Since God never gives up hope on us, we cannot give up hope on those with whom we work. Some of us have experienced hope imparted by parent, teacher, coach, friend, relative or employer, someone who would not give up on us. Their hopes and beliefs for us were both comforting and motivating. What may be impossible for you is possible for God, and prayer powerfully releases that possibility. Hope is confident expectation that buoys our prayer life, our attitude, and our treatment of others.

Formula for hope: pray daily for your people and believe in them When a manager prays daily for the people he or she works with, hope can become influential and tangible. Philosopher Goethe said, "If we treat people as they ought (hope) to be, we help them become what they are capable of becoming."

Henry Drummond, in *The Greatest Thing in the World*, remarked, "if we try to elevate others, we shall soon see that success is in proportion to their belief of our belief (hope) in them. The respect of another is the first restoration of the self-respect man has lost, our ideal of what he is, becomes to him, the hope and pattern of what he may become."

There is no hope for success without mistakes Humorist Will Rogers stated this reality: "Good judgment comes from experience, and a lot of that comes from bad judgment."

Absolutely no one gets it right the first time, every time. In fact, most successful people claim they learned most from their failures - so failure is never seen as final. Employees are at their most vulnerable when they fail, so a manager's response to and treatment of failure is greatly magnified. When failure occurs, the manager's job is to revive hope by patiently reviewing the original objectives and measurable outcomes, examining actions taken and lessons learned, and then encouraging the employee to have another go, this time armed with truths based on hard-won experience, in essence, failure.

CONCLUSION:

Present Hope in Christ, Gift Wrapped In the Loving Treatment of Others

QUESTIONS:

1. What are your hopes for the individuals with whom you work?

2. What are your hopes for yourself?

3. How are these hopes articulated in terms of planned strategies?

See Appendix 2: In Five Steps, Design A Plan For 'Any' Issue

11

MANAGEMENT PRACTICE:
LOVE ALWAYS PERSEVERES

SUPPORT:

Webster's on **Persevere**: "persist in an undertaking despite counter influences, opposition or discouragement."

Scriptures: "Blessed is the one who perseveres under trial, because, having stood the test, that person will receive the crown of life that the Lord has promised to those who love him" (James 1:12). "Let us not become weary in doing good for at the proper time we will reap a harvest, if we do not give up" (Galatians 6:9). "We know that suffering produces perseverance; perseverance, character; and character, hope. And hope does not put us to shame" (Romans 5:3).

APPLICATION:

In one of his most memorable addresses, in 1941 during the early days of World War II, Sir Winston Churchill, speaking at Harrow School, which he attended as a boy, said, "never give in, never, never, never, never – in nothing, great or small, large or petty...." It was a brief message about perseverance that the British – and the Allies – had to fall back on many times during those dark days. Perseverance is also a hallmark for people of faith.

Until our last breath, God never gives up the promise of salvation. Consider the thief on the cross adjoining the one on which Jesus hung. The thief, guilty as charged, in his final hours on earth entered the kingdom of heaven by accepting Jesus Christ as Lord and Savior. We Christian managers also must persevere in prayer, entreating God on behalf of those with whom we work.

Our Christian Witness – persevere because we are a work-in-progress If ever there was a case for perseverance, Philip Graham Ryken makes it in his book, *Loving the Way Jesus Loves*, suggesting that we regularly substitute our name in place of "Love" for each of the 1 Corinthians 13 mandates – such as, "John is patient, John is kind, John is not self-seeking,...." That is easy to say, not as easy to do. Being the "John" in this example, I have a long way to go on every Love practice. As do we all. So let us admit that we are, as Christians, works-in-progress striving at different levels of application on the subject of incorporating love as a habitual, management and life practice.

CONCLUSION:

Never give up, never give up, never, never, never give up Persevere in love, because the results are worth your reason for being as an earthly representative of Jesus Christ. Jesus taught His disciples that they should "always pray and never give up...." (Luke 18:1). We should daily make it our goal to do the same.

QUESTIONS:

1. How would you evaluate yourself overall in terms of the traits presented in the Bible about what love truly is, not only personally but also in the workplace?

2. How have you reached this conclusion? Would it help to have an assessment tool?

3.   Rank yourself from 1 to 10 (10 being the best) for practicing each of the love mandates we have discussed. See Appendix 2: In Five Steps, Design a Plan for "Any" Issue. Then develop a plan for improvement in those areas.

Priority Plan	*Rank* 10 (BEST) - 1(NONE)
• Love is patient	_____
• Love is kind	_____
• Love does not envy	_____
• Love is not proud	_____
• Love is not rude	_____
• Love is not self-seeking	_____
• Love keeps no record of wrongs	_____
• Love does not delight in evil, but rejoices in the truth	_____
• Love always protects	_____
• Love always hopes	_____
• Love always perseveres	_____

APPENDIX 1:

Questions for Small Group Discussion and Implementation

MAKING THE MOST OF THE BOOK

Don't try it alone. Change happens best in community. That is the power of using the book in a small group or one-on-one relationship.

Be prepared. Read the section before your small group meets and respond to the personal reflection questions.

Read it again. Begin your small group discussion by re-reading the section out loud.

Focus the discussion. Use the small group discussion questions in the appendix to move everyone toward the application of the principles in their life. Don't rush the discussion. It may take several meetings to get where you want to go.

Ask good questions. Help others explore and clarify the changes they want to see happen in their personal situation. Don't give advice.

Listen well. You will learn more listening to others than by hearing yourself speak.

Pair up for growth. Accountability, and support are critical to successful change.

Practice #1

LOVE IS PATIENT

1. How has a leader in your work setting demonstrated this practice toward you? How did it impact you personally and professionally?

2. How have you demonstrated this practice in your work setting toward those you lead or influence?

3. What would be some specific things you could begin doing now to enhance your use of this practice as a management principle?

4. What would be some potential obstacles?

5. How could those obstacles be removed?

6. What help or accountability do you need from this group? Who in the group might be the best person to hold you accountable?

Practice #2

LOVE IS KIND

1. How has a leader in your work setting demonstrated this practice toward you? How did it impact you personally and professionally?

2. How have you demonstrated this practice in your work setting toward those you lead or influence?

3. What would be some specific things you could begin doing now to enhance your use of this practice as a management principle?

4. What would be some potential obstacles?

5. How could those obstacles be removed?

6. What help or accountability do you need from this group? Who in the group might be the best person to hold you accountable?

Practice #3

LOVE DOES NOT ENVY

1. How has a leader in your work setting demonstrated this practice toward you? How did it impact you personally and professionally?

2. How have you demonstrated this practice in your work setting toward those you lead or influence?

3. What would be some specific things you could begin doing now to enhance your use of this practice as a management principle?

4. What would be some potential obstacles?

5. How could those obstacles be removed?

6. What help or accountability do you need from this group? Who in the group might be the best person to hold you accountable?

Practice #4

LOVE IS NOT PROUD

1. How has a leader in your work setting demonstrated this practice toward you? How did it impact you personally and professionally?

2. How have you demonstrated this practice in your work setting toward those you lead or influence?

3. What would be some specific things you could begin doing now to enhance your use of this practice as a management principle?

4. What would be some potential obstacles?

5. How could those obstacles be removed?

6. What help or accountability do you need from this group? Who in the group might be the best person to hold you accountable?

Practice #5

LOVE IS NOT RUDE

1. How has a leader in your work setting demonstrated this practice toward you? How did it impact you personally and professionally?

2. How have you demonstrated this practice in your work setting toward those you lead or influence?

3. What would be some specific things you could begin doing now to enhance your use of this practice as a management principle?

4. What would be some potential obstacles?

5. How could those obstacles be removed?

6. What help or accountability do you need from this group? Who in the group might be the best person to hold you accountable?

Practice #6

LOVE IS NOT SELF SEEKING

1. How has a leader in your work setting demonstrated this practice toward you? How did it impact you personally and professionally?

2. How have you demonstrated this practice in your work setting toward those you lead or influence?

3. What would be some specific things you could begin doing now to enhance your use of this practice as a management principle?

4. What would be some potential obstacles?

5. How could those obstacles be removed?

6. What help or accountability do you need from this group? Who in the group might be the best person to hold you accountable?

Practice #7

LOVE KEEPS NO RECORDS OF WRONGS

1. How has a leader in your work setting demonstrated this practice toward you? How did it impact you personally and professionally?

2. How have you demonstrated this practice in your work setting toward those you lead or influence?

3. What would be some specific things you could begin doing now to enhance your use of this practice as a management principle?

4. What would be some potential obstacles?

5. How could those obstacles be removed?

6. What help or accountability do you need from this group? Who in the group might be the best person to hold you accountable?

Practice #8

LOVE DOES NOT DELIGHT IN EVIL, BUT REJOICES IN THE TRUTH

1. How has a leader in your work setting demonstrated this practice toward you? How did it impact you personally and professionally?

2. How have you demonstrated this practice in your work setting toward those you lead or influence?

3. What would be some specific things you could begin doing now to enhance your use of this practice as a management principle?

4. What would be some potential obstacles?

5. How could those obstacles be removed?

6. What help or accountability do you need from this group? Who in the group might be the best person to hold you accountable?

Practice #9

LOVE ALWAYS PROTECTS

1. How has a leader in your work setting demonstrated this practice toward you? How did it impact you personally and professionally?

2. How have you demonstrated this practice in your work setting toward those you lead or influence?

3. What would be some specific things you could begin doing now to enhance your use of this practice as a management principle?

4. What would be some potential obstacles?

5. How could those obstacles be removed?

6. What help or accountability do you need from this group? Who in the group might be the best person to hold you accountable?

Practice #10

LOVE ALWAYS HOPES

1. How has a leader in your work setting demonstrated this practice toward you? How did it impact you personally and professionally?

2. How have you demonstrated this practice in your work setting toward those you lead or influence?

3. What would be some specific things you could begin doing now to enhance your use of this practice as a management principle?

4. What would be some potential obstacles?

5. How could those obstacles be removed?

6. What help or accountability do you need from this group? Who in the group might be the best person to hold you accountable?

Practice #11

LOVE ALWAYS PERSEVERES

1. How has a leader in your work setting demonstrated this practice toward you? How did it impact you personally and professionally?

2. How have you demonstrated this practice in your work setting toward those you lead or influence?

3. What would be some specific things you could begin doing now to enhance your use of this practice as a management principle?

4. What would be some potential obstacles?

5. How could those obstacles be removed?

6. What help or accountability do you need from this group? Who in the group might be the best person to hold you accountable?

APPENDIX 2:
IN FIVE STEPS, DESIGN A PLAN FOR 'ANY' ISSUE

Principle: *Measurability clarifies hope and determines achievement*

1. **Issue**: Name an opportunity for OR obstacle to GROWTH in a particular area.

2. **Importance**:
    a. Describe 3 negative consequences of failure to resolve this issue:

    1)

    2)

    3)

    b. Describe 3 positive consequences of resolving this issue:

    1)

    2)

    3)

3. **Solution**: Describe the very best outcomes for this issue, as measured by specific, understood criteria:
    a. Outcome A ... as measured by ...

    b. Outcome B ... as measured by ...

    c. Outcome C ... as measured by ...

    d. etc.

    (Remember, measurability clarifies hope and determines achievement.)

4. **Resolution**: Name 5 possible obstacles standing in way of your Solution, each expressed as a challenge by starting with the words 'How to' ...

   a. How to ... better manage my time

   b. How to ... secure financial support

   c. How to ... attract partners

   d. How to ... obtain buy-in from my people

   e. How to ... create a sense of urgency

   Obstacles may arise from lack of:
   - Funding
   - Systems, technology, facilities
   - Sense of urgency, available time
   - Knowledge, information, skills, training
   - Culture, incentive to change
   - Available capable leadership
   - Research required
   - Support from suppliers, consultants, others
   - "Pucker factors" – performance guarantees

5. **Action Plan**: Attack the least challenging obstacle first. Here's an example for how to go about it. It might be, "How to" better manage my time.

   Steps:
   1) Current status – "distracted"; desired status – "focused"

   2) Action steps leading to "focused"

      a. Daily list "to do's"

      b. Prioritize "to do's"

    c. Day end check items "done"

    d. Carry forward items "undone"

    e. Take time management training

Next: Having made progress, engage a more challenging obstacle, building confidence as you successfully proceed toward the overall Solution to your Issue. Related obstacles will emerge as you "peel the onion" and remove specific impediments.

Caution: Ambitiously attacking several Obstacles at the same time is not advised. Because special projects are always superimposed on full work schedules, demanding extra time and effort to complete. Consequently, you run the very real risk of becoming overwhelmed, leading to discouragement and ultimately, abandoning the project altogether. This is a common reason for strategic plan failure.

> (Now this advice is moot if the project deals with a drop-dead emergency. Then you do all you can, the best you can. Once the emergency has passed, you can return to attacking the opportunity for – or obstacle to – growth.)

BIOGRAPHY: John E. Johnson

- HBA Western University (Canada's Harvard Business School)

- 8 years, Marketing Brand Management, Unilever, Canada – consumer products

- 20 years, Advertising Management - sole client, Levi Strauss & Co, USA, all apparel

- 14 years, Chair, Vistage Worldwide* - Chair Emeritus

- 16 years, Subject Expert Speaker ** - Vistage rated "Exceptional"

- Married 58 years to one great wife with four loving daughters and their families

- Spiritual mission: To Glorify God by revealing Jesus Christ, gift wrapped in love

*Vistage Worldwide; world's largest association of CEOs. As chair, I worked one-to-one monthly with 30+ entrepreneurial California CEOs, then facilitated 2 to 3 all-day monthly group meetings processing CEO issues

** Invented "The 60-Minute Strategic Plan" implemented by 10,000 CEOs in 700 worldwide workshops. Published in 2006, "The 60-Minute Strategic Plan" continues to be available on Amazon.com

John E. Johnson
805-770-3974
JohnJohnsonDavis@gmail.com

Made in the USA
Monee, IL
06 November 2020